I Can Read About™

Alligators and Crocodiles

Written by David Knight • Illustrated by Pamela G. Johnson

*Consultant: Dr. Edmund D. Brodie, Jr., Professor and Head,
Department of Biology, Utah State University*

Troll

Watch out! It's an alligator. *Snap!* The alligator's powerful jaws shut upon its prey.

Like its close relative the crocodile, the alligator has a mouth filled with sharp teeth. These teeth, along with strong jaws, make alligators and crocodiles ferocious hunters.

Alligators and crocodiles belong to a group of animals called *reptiles.* Other reptiles include snakes, lizards, and turtles. Like all reptiles, alligators and crocodiles have backbones and lungs to breathe air.

All reptiles, including alligators and crocodiles, share another trait. They are cold-blooded animals. This means that their body temperatures change along with the temperature of the surrounding air or water. This is different from warm-blooded animals, whose temperatures stay about the same no matter what the surrounding temperature is.

Alligators and crocodiles are members of the *crocodilian* (krah-kuh-DIH-lee-in) family. Other crocodilians include the gharial and the caiman.

Crocodile

Alligator

Caiman

Gharial

The crocodilians make up one of the oldest families of reptiles surviving on Earth today. The ancestors of today's crocodilians lived at the same time as the dinosaurs—millions of years ago. Some of these ancestors from long ago were twice as long as modern-day crocodiles.

Champsosaurus

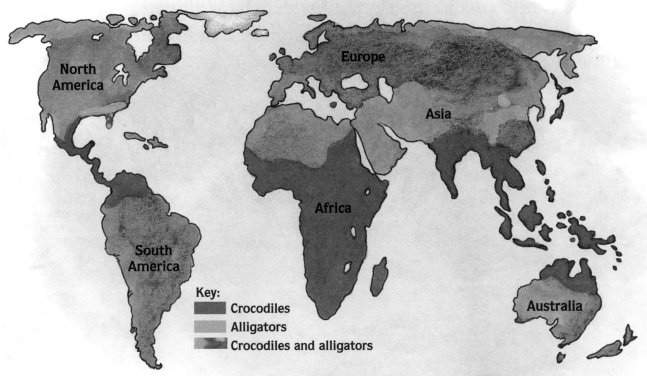

Locations of crocodilians

North America

Europe

Asia

Africa

South America

Australia

Key:
Crocodiles
Alligators
Crocodiles and alligators

Crocodilians are found in many places throughout the world. Most alligators live in North America, although there is one kind that lives in China.

Crocodiles are more widespread than alligators. Most live in tropical places, such as Africa, India, Malaysia, and Australia.

13

There is one area in the United States where alligators and crocodiles live together. It is in the swampy marshland of southern Florida.

As for the other crocodilians, the caiman lives in Central and South America. Caimans are strong swimmers. Some have huge, shiny eyes. They almost look as if they are wearing eyeglasses.

Caimans

The gharial lives in Asia. This crocodilian has a skinny head with strong jaws and sharp teeth.

Gharial

Alligators and crocodiles are closely related. They look very much alike. Both have tough hides made of bony plates. Both have webbed feet and are good swimmers. And both can move about on land, as well as in the water. In addition, both alligators and crocodiles have strong jaws that are filled with sharp teeth.

Alligator

Crocodile

Although they are alike in many ways, it is possible to tell alligators and crocodiles apart. Look closely at their snouts. Do you see a difference? A fully grown American alligator's snout is broad, while an American crocodile's snout is thin and pointed.

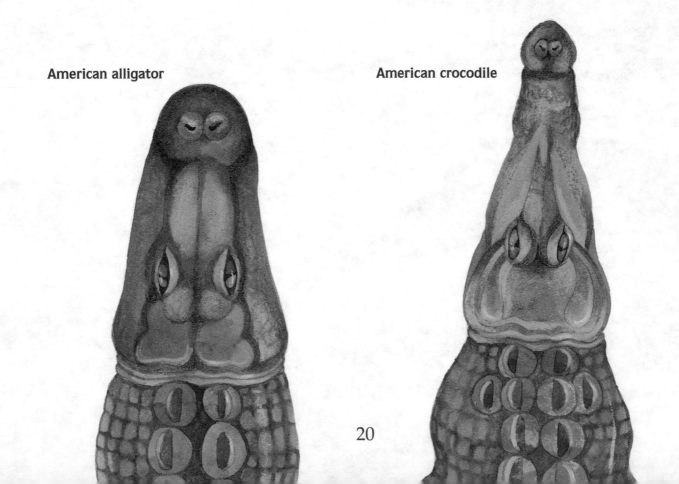

American alligator

American crocodile

Another difference is evident when a crocodile and an alligator close their jaws. Only some of the top teeth of the alligator can be seen. The crocodile is different. Both its upper and lower teeth are visible. In fact, the crocodile looks almost as if it is grinning. But don't let that fool you—crocodiles have nasty tempers!

Crocodile

Alligator

On land, both alligators and crocodiles use their strong legs to run short distances. They sometimes run surprisingly fast. But these animals prefer the water. They swish their powerful tails from side to side when they swim.

Alligators and crocodiles often look like dead tree trunks floating in the water. Their eyes and nostrils stick up above the surface. In this way, these reptiles can easily see and surprise their prey.

Crocodiles and alligators can stay under water for a long time. These animals have special flaps that close off the nose, throat, and ears in order to keep water out.

The jaws of alligators and crocodiles are very, very strong. With one mighty crunch, these reptiles can snap a large branch in two. But the muscles that open the jaws are very weak. A strong person can hold the jaws of an alligator or crocodile shut with his or her bare hands. Hunters sometimes catch these animals for zoos in this way.

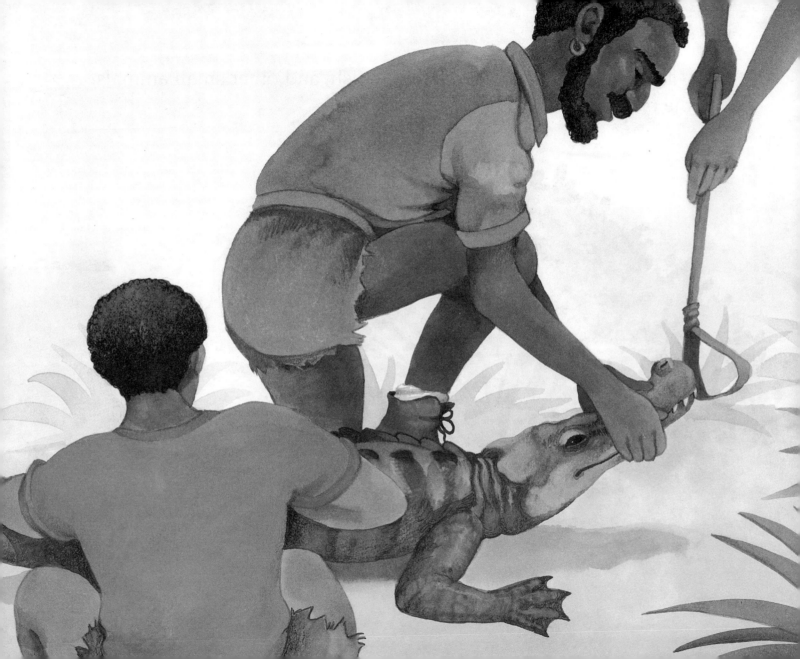

Alligators and crocodiles eat birds, fish, and other small animals.
If the prey is small, it is swallowed whole.

Sometimes crocodiles and alligators attack larger animals. They drag their prey into the water and drown it. Then they tear the dead animal into pieces that are small enough to swallow.

Alligators and crocodiles cannot chew their food. To help them digest, these animals swallow stones. As the stones bump together in their stomachs, the food is broken up.

Alligators and crocodiles are similar in another way. Like most reptiles, they lay eggs. Their eggs have tough shells.

A female alligator makes a large nest out of mud, leaves, and grass. Then she lays her eggs, covers them, and stands guard nearby. After they hatch, the mother may carry the babies in her mouth to bring them to the water. She stays with the babies for about a year to keep them safe.

A mother crocodile deposits her eggs in the sand. Like the alligator, she guards them until she hears the babies. As they push out of their shells, they make a grunting sound. Then the mother quickly uncovers them.

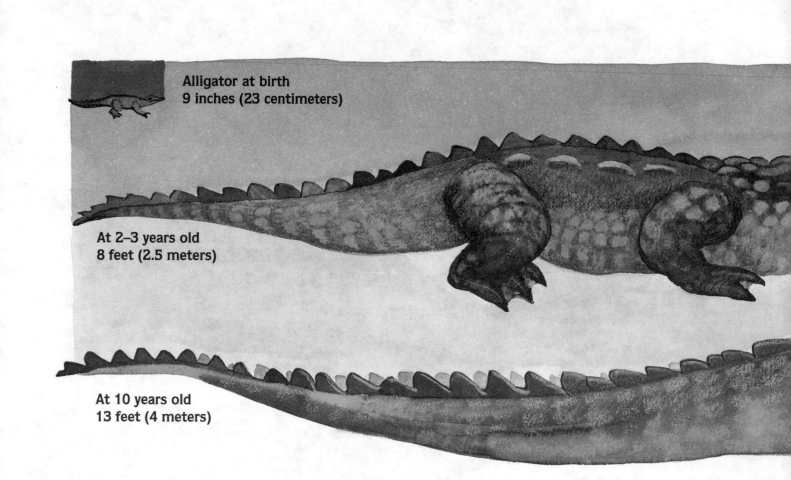

Alligator at birth
9 inches (23 centimeters)

At 2–3 years old
8 feet (2.5 meters)

At 10 years old
13 feet (4 meters)

Baby alligators and crocodiles are 9 inches (23 centimeters) long when they hatch. It takes several years for them to reach their full adult size. Most alligators grow to be about 8 feet (2.5 meters) long, but some have grown as long as 13 feet (4 meters).

Alligators have a long life span. They may live as long as sixty years.

American crocodiles are usually longer than alligators, but they are not as heavy. These crocodiles also move more quickly and are more likely to attack humans than many alligators.

Nile crocodiles

The American crocodile grows to a length of about 12 feet (3.7 meters). The Nile crocodile grows to about 18 feet (5.5 meters) in length. It is found in Africa, except in the dry Sahara and in the north along the coast. The longest crocodile ever found was from India. It was over 33 feet (10 meters) long.

Crocodiles do not live as long as alligators. Scientists believe this reptile's life span is from twenty to thirty years.

Alligators and crocodiles make all kinds of sounds. They bellow, grunt, and croak. But there are times when they remain silent.

One of these times is when they are lying
in the water waiting for their next meal.

When there is a long, hot, dry spell, or when the weather gets too cold, crocodiles and alligators dig down into the mud until they are buried. Their breathing and heartbeat get very, very slow. These reptiles enter a sleeplike state until the conditions change and it is time for them to become active again.

In the past, alligators were common in many parts of the United States. But so many were killed that laws were passed to protect them. More recently, the population of American alligators has increased, and some hunting of these animals is allowed.

Alligators and crocodiles are fascinating creatures. The next time you see one at the zoo, try to discover if it is an alligator or a crocodile. Look carefully—but don't get too close!

Index

Africa, 13, 41
alligators:
    ability to stay underwater, 26
    differences from crocodiles, 20,
        21, 40, 41
    effect of surrounding
        temperatures on, 9, 44
    food eaten by, 30
    jaws and teeth of, 5, 6, 18, 21, 28
    laws to protect, 45
    life span of, 39
    locations of, 13, 14
    movements of, 22
    nest of, 35
    populations of, 45
    protecting nest and babies, 35
    similarities to crocodiles, 6, 8, 9,
        18, 23, 26, 30, 34, 42, 44
    size of, 38–39
    snout of, 20
    sounds made by, 42
American crocodile, 40, 41
Asia, 17
Australia, 13

babies, 35, 36, 39
backbones, 8
birds, 30
body temperature, 9
bony plates, 18
breathing, 8, 44

caiman, 10, 11, 16
Central America, 16
Champsosaurus, 12
China, 13
cold-blooded animals, 9
cold weather, 44
crocodiles:
    ability to stay underwater, 26

behavior of mothers, 36
differences from alligators, 20,
    21, 40, 41
digestion of, 33
effect of surrounding
    temperatures on, 9, 44
food eaten by, 30
jaws and teeth of, 6, 18, 21
life span of, 41
locations of, 13, 14
movements of, 22
similarities to alligators, 6, 8, 9,
    18, 23, 26, 30, 34, 42, 44
size of, 40–41
snout of, 20
sounds made by, 42
crocodilians, 10, 12, 13, 16, 17
    ancestors of, 12
    locations of, 13, 16, 17

dinosaurs, 12
dry spell, 44

ears, 26
eggs, 34, 35, 36
    hatching of, 35, 39
    shells of, 34, 36
eyes, 16, 24

fish, 30
Florida, 14

gharial, 10, 11, 17
grass, 35

head, 17
heartbeat, 44
hides, 18
hunters, 6, 28, 45

India, 13, 41

land, 18, 22
leaves, 35
legs, 22
lizards, 8
lungs, 8

Malaysia, 13
marshland, 14
mud, 35

nest, 35
Nile crocodile, 41
North America, 13
nose and nostrils, 24, 26

prey, 5, 24, 30, 32

reptiles, 8, 9, 12, 24, 28, 34, 43, 44
    traits of, 8, 9

Sahara, 41
sand, 36
snakes, 8
snouts, 20
South America, 16
stomach, 33
swallowing, 30, 33
swimming, 16, 18, 22

tails, 22
throat, 26
turtles, 8

United States, 14, 45

warm-blooded animals, 9
water, 9, 18, 22, 24, 26, 32, 35, 43
webbed feet, 18

zoos, 28, 46